CORINA

by Cori Lark

Copyright © 2010 by Cori Lark

ISBN 978-0-7414-4284-0

Printed in the United States of America
Published May 2004

INFINITY PUBLISHING
1094 New DeHaven Street, Suite 100
West Conshohocken, PA 19428-2713
Toll-free (877) BUY BOOK
Local Phone (610) 941-9999
Fax (610) 941-9959
Info@buybooksontheweb.com
www.buybooksontheweb.com

I Welcome

1- Red Ink

2- On My Way

3-The Muse In Me

4- Grounding

5- I Am Bits and Grams Measured

6- Becoming Osprey

7- Son Of A Bitch

8- Crazy Love

9- Read Me

II Whispering Windows

1- Reflections

2- Talk

3- Little Bear

4- Guided By A Whispering Pen Waiting
        For The Next Word

5- I Put My Clothes On And Left

6- We Shall Find Our Way

7- Once Upon A Letter--A Halloween Reply

8- Rest In Peace

9- Send Now II

10- Blank Brain

III If You Dare

1- May '03

2- Psychopathic Superqueerdo

3- Autumn '03

4- Fall 2003

5- 1/3/04

6- Let's Open Up Our Eyes And Breathe

7- Blank Girl Walking

8- L.G.

9- Channel 12 News

10- Crazy, Sexy, Cool

11- Vernacular Apathy

12- Calandra DaVaki

13- Cryptic Cries

14- Lyrics

15- Carinna

16- Friendly Lover

IV <u>Alfresco Activities</u>

1- Toward Jeweled Design

2- Travels

3- 5/08/04 (poemprayer)

4- Los Redi

5- Heart Healers

6- Gebo

7- Mannaz Reversed

8- Wunjo Reversed

9- Berkana Reversed

10- Raido

V <u>In The End, There Was Just One</u>

1- Stringless Bikini

2- 2004CM55555

3- The Ring

4- A Note

5- Breathless Vibes

6- Psychic Bondage of Three Women

7- Witching Hour

8- Phantom Lives, a song

9- Morning After Union Station

10- Note #2, June

11- I Wish Him Peace, As I Bleed

12- Friday Night

13- Muse

14- Searching For The Highest Cloud

15- Currents of Wind Surfing On Silver Rain

16- Warming Up After Being Stoned Cold

17- Old Friend

18-Strength

I <u>Welcome</u>

I-1
Red Ink

On a journey
we proceed
through the journal
of empty dreams
On this sacred ground
I bleed
Spilling out
bleeding ink
now you will hear
my melody
rhyme with me
read me raw
take a pound
I'll give you more
Hear my sound
Don't resist
my roar--
No hiding out--
I explore...
Feed the ink
the bright color--
Hear me speak--
walk through
the door.

I-2
On My Way

I taste lies
brewed by the life in this time
Spit out in solitude
seeing dreams of distant lands.
Where is my blissful ignorance?
This mind still journeys
like an eagle's dance
with only the sound of the wind
singing hymes unheard from earth.
Here I am.
Once I swam in my lake
Now I drown in their sea.
May the sun warm my soul
May the soil cleanse my grief.
I must find my place.
So mote it be.

The Muse In Me

More welcomed than a lover's touch
More treasured than a jeweled home
We waltz on water
when you enter my soul.
She sent you to me--
I thank you, indeed.
You've come just in time--
I've waited in need.
Through the mist
is a path--
with the wind,
through the trees--
not a search but a flight
to a garden that breathes.
Hold my hand,
as I will,
our words lead--
take us to Avalon
So mote it be.

I-4
Grounding

I have to go back
my heart still beats
Though, here in this page
full of colors
I breathe.
When I return
may I please keep
you in my heart,
my steps to your beat.
Protect me from harm
with your light
may I see.
At night, when I sleep
may you enter my dreams.
Clear my path
with your wind
through the days, may I breathe.
Keep near my soul
With your water
I'm clean.
Nourish my body
your fruit I will eat.
Help me to live
So mote it be.

I Am Bits And Grams Measured

I am bits and grams measured five times
        within a smoky mind.
To have a love awaiting you...
        the evening is of two
In rest, in bed, nocturnal beat--
Nightmares to warn of doom—
It's true. It's nice. Disguising life
        or making lovers blind...
Libido jumps—glance at his butt
        In lusting thoughts gone wild
belly crashes bucking faster as
together gripping grind...
The fantasies intruding me...
I welcome sexy mind—
But controlling steps walk past
I already miss that ass...
So love is great perfectly made--
        I'm pretty satisfied...
I like it but I need to jump,
the seasons sing their rhymes.
I want a balanced life—
I can't make up my mind—
I'm running out of time—
Goddess be in my life.

I-6
Becoming Osprey

The osprey
bent back her wing
took a dive
wheels rolling
she didn't plunge
but traveled on
slim silhouette
soars far from
the shoreline daze
to swampy tides
a new migrate
a quiet life.
Eyes in focus
zooming in
fresh water swamp
Spring air opens
A mystic drumming
sounds below
Circling
High and low
the common snipe
her zigzag flight
flying by
the osprey finds
the pulsing girl
is very shy.

I see her flutter
through osprey eyes
I'll chirp and mutter
She'll run and hide
I surrender to nervous cries
Flying on to
new sunrise.

I-7
Son of a Bitch, a parody

First let me tell you, I'm fucken crazy—
Unto the page I am creating—
Causing my mind—to escape me—
Keep on breathing—my screams release me—

Edgy Addictions—bleed from my fingers—
Nothing in this world—will get in my way—

Somingthin's comin' out, I wanna work my fingers—
On and on I puff while the smoke lingers—
Night comes around and takes a hold of me—
Off I will go in and out of these dreams—

From birth to death I'll sing this poetry—
Another year, it floats above me—

Bass beats on and on—I must surrender—
In poetic song, I must explain—
The mirrors of life—hate and love me—
Causing the day to fall far from me—

How does this S.O.B--keep on living?…

I-8
Crazy Love

My many personalities
might move around your love for me
like ocean waves or hurricanes
windy whirling-- love and hate.

You must admit
You're guilty, too--
Our games and songs
with voices crude--
All of this, and right next to
Your voice,
at times,
it speaks the truth.

I cannot be your diary
But I'd like to hear a song so sweet
true as in your hand writing
your
Personalities.

Read Me

I read like the mountains read the wind…
I cannot read in a moving vehicle. My eyes cross, the letters turn green and purple, my brain begins to ache, and whatever is in my stomach journeys outside gravity.

I read masterpieces of literature!
I open the book on a nice day, sitting on the porch, smelling the green that surrounds me, wishing my ass didn't hurt so much from sitting and sitting, reading on, page by wonderful page while the neighbors jog by with their dogs, while children chase after Frisbees. I disappear into the print and forget that my ass hurts and that people, cars, and flowers surround me, until my mother turns the porch light on because the sun is setting against colorful sky and it's bad for your eyes if you read in the dark. Then all of a sudden I absorb the last word, return to the porch, and hear the crickets chirping through dark lawn and quiet brush.

I read trashy words.
I study the characters, the plot, the scenery within each boring page and wonder what perspective I would have written that story or what other characters could be added to make up for the weak story line and cliché imagery. Then, after two, maybe three chapters, I toss the grocery store paperback aside and only pick the damn waste of money and

waste of paper up again to give it back to the old friend who thought I might like it.

I read everything. Once your first grade teacher teaches you how to read, there is no turning back. Painted words on dumpsters call to me, printed letters on tin cans want me to kiss them, billboards want me to get into a car accident, stop signs want me to stop, and so does the Diary Queen down on Main Street...

I read textbooks. I sit on my couch, smoking my cigarettes, drinking my black Italian Roast coffee, with my highlighter in my right hand. I decipher important sentence from not so important sentence. Then my cat plops his belly smack dab in the middle of my open text, next to my smelly ashtray. His tail rubs against my coffee cup. He looks up at me wanting some TLC, and we wait for spring so we can say hello to my porch again.

I read poetry.
And witty verse--leaning into the book, my eyes, blood-thirsty.

II <u>Whispering Windows</u>

II-1
Reflections

A child-
horny for excitement,
willingly naïve,
embraces every emotion.
Driven toward love
by hopes of more love
shoots into puberty—
like a bat on the hunt—
fearless—
free—

She traveled
through mist
searching for the moonlight—
but, the paths turned shady,
the nights were dark.

Now, it sleeps within her, waiting,
while her soul, trying to balance,
sitting on the edge
of tomorrow,
dreams …

It sprinkles her magick here,
where the forces of nature are free ...
This is where She met him
where their needs were born--
where they now release--
Here, *you are you--*
        I am me—

He is her moonlight
Reflected--
reaching toward her--
She can feel him
if she lets herself see.

Sorry
She is not free
of daily maiming
helpless psyche.
If only
she could give to him
what he would give to her ...
Hoping that time will give
intrinsic needs of three.

Talk

You haunt me?
It may be true—
I blunder through the day
And then there you are—
I wonder how, why, what and how far…

Have you cast a spell?
Do you enter my sleep?
Is it your flesh I dream?
Do you call out to me?

Such sweet words you whisper
They too, do burn—
And tickle and hurt
Again, do I yearn?

You speak of a moment known—
Which one is that?
I do not cherish
that one evening past.

A kitchen without patience
Turn the clocks back…
Stranger, we cooked up
Classical and rap.

Our rhythm is written
We could learn to dance
Beyond the pen
Is a dream, beyond the dream
is
the end

unless someone acts.

Little Bear

Little Bear
Cautious and quiet
I hear the wisdom in your words
Your mind, body and spirit
Teach me of your strength
And your courage
Your magick mind wound
Your heart beats on strong
Firm and fearless sounds
The truth within your song
I see with each new moon
Your insight awakens
Your endurance blesses you
With the knowledge of the sacred
Your spirit lives on
As does my love for you

II-4

Guided By A Whispering Pen Waiting For The Next Word

Perhaps I shall switch to the bottle.

Please, and make that not the only switch...

Why—to what are you referring, kind sir?

I am referring, madam, to your choice of companions.

Your bold words, my lord, leave me to believe you have an interest in whom I am intimate, to whom I give my attention.

I seem to have all of it, at the moment.

This is true.
We converse, but...

What?

I am promised to another.

And she walks away
While his words, weaving with the wind,
Whisper, *You should not be promised at all—*
Your beauty, it is but one of your powers, my dear.

Her pace slows,
He states full and clear,
Your heart will guide you
Right into my arms,
my dear.

She turns around
To face his eyes
The sunshine blinds

And he is gone.

I Put My Close On And Left

Ninety-eight pages
in sixty-eight minutes
It went so fast
I wanted more.
Two tingles
did tickle my trip
but before I could taste
each word from the core.
Is it me?
The fast read?
I couldn't see--,
couldn't see me.
I didn't feel anger
seeping out from your pores…
I should read the old one
But still I wait
Who knows how long
I'll procrastinate
At any rate,
I'd like to continue this poem.
Where is your truth?
Have you found your way?
Are you lost inside a maze in your brain?
I guess this is goodbye
I tried
I tried

and now we're left
with a white empty page
when we both expected
so much
more.

II-6
We Shall Find Our Way

Over and over and over again
Burning away—Dying in vain
I'm up and I'm down
Rage Love and Hate
wrestling peace—healing fate.
Over and over and over again
In and out of this place
and that face
I race on and on and on again—

Are you my friend
yodeling from the hillside?

I race—
In a craze
Burning away
Searching minutes and days
Praying to my heavenly guides
We shall find our way.

Once Upon A Letter--A Halloween Reply

Thou art a true poet.
All that I know and feel of artful words is exemplified
through your pen.
Calling me forth again,
I feel a need to bring
down mine pen
however,
mine fingertips would rather gently caress
keys for words true.
Indeed, an advantage emerges. Blessed abilities of
computers...

On page one, your words fly past mine eyes, force a smile
unto mine lips.
And on and on with each turn
I discover the words I miss...
Do you have a magick pool? Day two begins
You brightened up my graying heart
Although you're drunk again--
You sweep through me, words brush my soul
like Vampire corporality mixed with spiritual--
Baton Rouge orchestra
Singing in my ears
a great friend and a wonderful dream
will last throughout the years...
You amaze me then make me giggle.

You wake me up, line-by-line, enhancing my sensations.
And now I long to be with the Gypsy hermits
you suggest in your rhyme…
Layers of Blue and lavender between thick strips of peach
and pink,
with shadows of maples and oaks on the horizon
resting in peace…

It is snowing!
It's October!
It is the Witching Hour
Let's go back to 1827 for just a moment.
A cold and windy night.
Edgar crouches beside grave
upon which there is no name
no fancy engrave
but blankness on its slate.
Tired shadows resting still
beneath the moonlight
The wind gusts through
the tree whistles
scraping branches against pine
Leaves of oak dance down the grass
A howl
heard through the night.
He stands fighting with the wind
walking over graves gone blind
to a maple tree, he sits
waiting hypnotized

wind calms quite breeze around thee
his silence becomes dead
as the chilly mist surrounds thee.
Why—

"Hellfire and Bloody Damnation!" Why? Why? Why?
Boy, drug talk is boring now
But Sex--sweet and soft
or rough and sticky Erotica?
Try not to get lost.
A tri-sexual- don'tchya know- will try anything once
Now me, I have my limits
I just want to fuck
Me beneath my bed sheet plus
A few roses on pillows
Driving my libido up into secret gardens…
Would you like a taste?
Don't let it go to waste.
Enough said.
I'll go take that bath.
Good journeys.
Write me back.
The Mad God,
He is spunky! Mad!
I'm on page 32
I feel lucky
to have a friend like you
… to read on is all to do!!!!!!!
Do you talk to all girls that way?

Wouldn't matter anyway
The words I have still glow…
I smoked 1 1/2 J's last night
instead of my regular 3
and a dolphin swam through my soul…
like a Tchaikovsky melody
I love to sleep. I love to dream.

Double bubble Smooth and subtle Cauldron's burning I'm in trouble.
I finally figured out what they really mean when they say
Love is Blind.
After a drink of your blood, I find myself afloat extremely high…
Woe is me, what am I to do? I've been throbbing for days,
thinking of …

Spirits will be coming out to play
wisdom at the crossroads
in howling wind, prophesy done
Celtic festival--
The veil at its thinnest point
The souls of the dead
come into the land of the living.
I offer cakes and bread.
Good day, my friend.
This is
the end.

Rest In Peace

Vronsky died while I… oh, I'm not
sure what I was doing at the time.
At any whine… I cry.
So now what?
But wait,
he lives
In page thirty-four—
I must read on
I must see more…
Okay,
So I never really knew
Him to begin with,
but I think he died by eighty-three.
I hate it when guys lie to me.
No, no—that's not it.
Writers are loony.
No, not loony,
But nuts,
Not nuts,
But crazy—insane! Gaga! Possessed! Definitely unstable in
some way…
Yeah-that's it.
But I already knew that.

Send Now II

I feel like whispering a slow song
Admitting battles go on and on
My findings in improvising
May lead to an early grave...
Anyway, I wanted to say
It is not that I had a bad day
But rather a busy one
Startled by ringing rain...
I have a message
I will communicate
In this here melody
We may consummate
No, really, it's just a note
To let you know of an envelope
It's sealed and it is for you
I'll leave it where I always do
Have smiles this day--
Friend, I hope you peace,
no pain.

II-10
Blank Brain

Blank Brain
Will not let
me explain
Three Hundred Sixty five days…
I still hold my pain—

I don't hold it on my sleeve
It lies beneath
down deep
in me
at times I feel
it creeps up on me—
I hold my breath
sore throat,
eyes wet—
Push it down
Were love has drowned…

memories of madness
those days--
love
sadness
dramatic
expansive
my soul
it danced

and danced
and danced…

I tripped upon my sadness
trammeled in my happenings
with too many mentalities
Genuine tragedy

Today I sit the same—
But these days,
they have brought change
all over every place…
yet I remain--
silent
with my blank brain.

III If You Dare

III-1
May '03

A lunar eclipse evening past
Three ways balanced
Eyes open, I am.
See lights of nature
Raining for days
Smooth minutes
Tick away…

The witch within me
Seeks nature and truths
My questions have answers
I need my free will…

As neurotic *Jars of Clay*
Tell me to fly far away
I pray…
They say they'll repair me
But I cannot be fixed
I'm a broken clock
Out of tock, out of tick…

Give me the night
Give me the day
Make my dreams hopeful
Show me my way…

III-2
Psycoslappeth Superqueerdo

Masochistic
Maddened misfit
Mind-controlled
By time--
Blackening by
bong-drift daze
with cigarette
and wine.

The news
It makes her want to shoot herself
Bamb!
All is blank
She'd fuck that up
She'd fucking live
In media
Maze--
Watch
herself
On the tube
in her nose
out her poop
Dead at last
Dead Times two.

Demented poem
of decadence
Drowning in her smoke
It kisses her
Makes her smile
Then makes her fucking choke.
It entertains
Day by day
'till life becomes a joke.
She says it loud
but She's not proud
Addict-wimp-
can't cope--.
So on and on they take a hit
a drag,
a hearty toke.
She asks herself for something else,
But always answers, "nope."
It's truly fun
It really is
So sweet, the Chardonnay
The cigarette
The sticky
Green--
Feel it resonate
All is gone
On she falls
Lost for her free will…
It's there-- it is--

She must like this,
Masochistic
kill.

III-3
Autumn '03

I received a call
Well, a message really,
He had called
At a quarter past three
On Sunday morning
While I was soundly
in my bed
fast asleep--
Whathe f---!?
I thought he said...
I thought
he quit the drink!

Thank you, Goddess, I have landed.
There might be some permanent damage.
My karma, I must learn to manage.
My mind, I must learn to bandage.

Moxie words in long letters
Can lead me to my grave—
I read and write and live this life
Hoping to be saved.

Cig break
Countdown
To a four day sleep—

III-4
Fall 2003

Soldiers are dying
Fucken terrorists!
Sergeants, lieutenants
No pacifists
People forgetting
Caring less and less
Until they're told of their brother's friend's death.

III-5
1/3/04

Beauty in clear cries
Citing chimes in the city
Beating time upon the year

III-6
Let's Open Up Our Eyes and Breathe

Now I'm going to face it
Within my stoner bliss
I bleed this ink to you
Beginning with a list
The rooster crows
Train whistle blows
Crimson groans escape dry lips
Cat puke blunder
Cranky slumber
Now our day begins--
Stumbling out—
Sitting down—
Smoky urine—
Trickling out…
Then back to bed
To dream dark clouds…
Let's take a breather
In and out
The smoke lingers
Around—about—
Resinated chests
Our lungs don't rest
Thirty years
They help us smell
They help us live
On earth we yell

Hear our screams
The sticking green
We love
We hate
Back to bed…
It knocks me out
To sleep
To wheeze
Again wake up
Look in my face
Or turn away
Time catches up
Time is today
I don't know how
We last this long—
The next revolution
Has just become.
Your angry heart
It makes me weep
I need myself
I need to see.
Let's open up our eyes
And breathe.

Blank Girl Walking

Then smoke the shit!

Then you cook it!

But this

But that

I'll prove you wrong

Lyrics spoken-- a wicked song.

I used to feel—now I float.

I have a box

I am enclosed...

I hear the anger—intense as fire

Spewing out lips,

Blowing out nose—

A dragon burning from within

Mean as a blizzard

Hail three-inches-thick...

Farting all the while, here we go...

With invisible dick, stroke and stroke.

Do you want to be a six foot prick?...

Life is not a joke.

...vocal out, wake me up

churning smoke   mumble fuck

then you ask "What the hell or what the fuck

is the matter with you!"

Pig Latin!

Slut!

I do not speak

I just stand up
I'm in my box
The doors are shut
Walk away
I cannot take
One more wave
Of this hate
freely opened
And let escape
Utway the uckfay
And one more spank!

But the spank I've learned to like
Just let me get you gagged and tied...
You see, I can assimilate
I must, to survive your space.

I will live—
I won't waste—
Look in the mirror
I dare you to wait.
We must take control of our fate.
I will not kill you
I will not rape
I will simply walk
My own pace
No more crawling
No more fakes
No stubborn wanting

No fight
No quakes
Blank girl walking
Toward her fate.

III-8
L. G.

He is my little man
He chose me as his own
Frisky-funny-handsome-cunning-
A perverted freak
A sassy sphinx
I call him Gigi
My French putty
He can put on show
Kissing mirror
My familiar
Speaks to me—he knows.
He loves his bro,
Smoke Joe
Tonners-Bear-Smokes.
Hair ball here
Cat toy there
They will always have a home.

III-9
Channel 12 News

Attention everyone!
Nuclear bombs are now on sale
Fifty Million- A Black Market Special!
The Swiss Engineer—
The US Sleeps—
Libya and Iran deal with
Kahn Research Laboratory—

Yes—It's too short
But you know TV
News reports
One Minute Thirty...

III-10
Crazy, Sexy, Cool

Artful lovemaking
Smooth-- engaging

Tribal Bemidji
always playing

Kitty cat welcoming
Discover the sensory
Spicy lingerings-
In-door tinglings
Triple-tone-satin
Sliding in waves—

Mediterranean maiden
Beneath the full moon
Juxtapose Latin
Accent as they move

Soft shadows coming
Around bedpost leg
Crawling on headboard
Dance down pillowcase…

Fiery desires
Calm into being
Spanish spear heater

Tribal Bemidji
Melting with maiden
Levitating
Sparrowing pleasure
Inside
new ecstasies.

Vernacular Apathy

I must be free to speak my mind
Instead, I find
I'm threatened.
Once I clung
We lingered on
Lost inside our friendship.
Now I open my mind
Slow, I see what we both hide...
We trap ourselves
We sit apart, yet
Side by side--
Speaking riddles
By day subliminal
By night...

Invading serum reveals

this nocturnal mind.

Tell me what you find,

For I can't see past this week--
This life has turned me blind--
I feel a scream
sneak up on me
Slowly, it will subside...

I open up my mind
That once was lost in time--
Though I fear—

What will I find?

III-12
Calandra DaVaki

A temptress scintillating
myriad of golden tones,
glowing flesh growing fresh
she is Pagan Angel,
The Countess can be summoned
Chant her name around the fire
Circle three times Call her name
But beware of what you find.
You must do this with a gift
You have only three tries--
You'll levitate by her will
Dance sexual-- another realm
Pleasure electrified--
Prepare to feel wild--
Within the cyclone of her mind...
But if you fail
and she likes you not
You'll be alone
Unable to touch
Unable to love
with Calandra's face
Branded to your heart
gripping at your mind.

III-13
Cryptic Cries

Cryptic cries
Bloodshot eyes
Coffee stains
Ashtrays
polluting
My life—

Pondering prophecies...
Which one is right?

Live by the hour—
Sleep every night.

The dreams are distracted
by daytime lies,
by this years routine
and last years life.
I want to scream the truth
I want to live and die
With one true wish
I do wish
I'll have my peace-of mind.

III-14
Lyrics

Whispers
Massaging
Memories
Into accepting minds
Kissing, blessing,
Addressing
Words that hold
They want to shine—
Waiting to be re-released—
Serenading in the blind—
Bold and braving truths do feast,
tick on borrowed time.

Befalling like epiphanies
Now they see
It's time
To face the facts
Don't look back
Don't let your mad go mind.

III-15
Carinna

Guardian Angel,
May I call on thee?
Your name—
I will find…

Carinna--
Come to me…
See my wasting fright
I feel it each day--
I dream it each night…
I ask you, please,
Walk by my side.

I am filling spaces
from which I
ran to hide.
I haunt myself
I am with ghosts
Hazy daze
of days
gone by.

Give me a nudge,
a jab, a punch,
something loud to wake me up
I'm scrawling down,

I'm praying out
from where guidance is much needed.
Give me the strength to live in time
Even if it's the last minute.

III-16
Friendly Lover

Just knowing him
gives me youth
reminds me
to have fun

Even when we're straight
when we're simply hanging out
talking of anything
without a beer to bring it out...
I enjoy his company
that's what it's about--
a man I find comforting
but still makes my heart skip
while sweet words
spring out
irresistible lips.

I feel like a woman
when he's in my bed
I'm free to give the love he seeks
and accept that which he gives.

Always,
the morning after--
I'm still in a trance--
I look into the mirror
and smile to myself.

IV Alfresco Activities

IV-1
Toward Jeweled Design

I wait to be unfettered—
free from scares embedded in my soul.
Unbodied in twilight
dipping in flight
past centuries
without a map
I'll fly
toward my ancestors' reverence
inside a sunrise
coral corridors
chastely sublime
bestowing a path
luring the wild
Sacred surrender
Hallowed arrival
Let me swim in your presence
in naked, natural…
lift me to heaven
to the water's crown
blue jewels shining
across anchored realms.

IV-2
Travels

Like the dream in an autumn
swamp. Golden-barren—
below branches wet
with whispers
from other worlds.

IV-3
5/08/04 (poemprayer)

I need to speak with Isis, please.
I'd like her to look after me.
My strength in time in balance be.
Noon whistle wakes birds to sing
Lend me wings, I'll fly the wind beats
Along with sunrise and what will be.
If I tumble, again I'll seek—
Life has many journeys—
Night has many dreams—
Midnight magick blessed
Beneath horned moonbeams.

IV-4
Los Redi

Sweating words—
Obstacles popping from blue ball-point
Lunar Queen guiding, giving
Days closer to home—
Isis, my Goddess, I am
Enlisted in Life
Returning to you with each sleep.

IV-5
Heart Healers

Following a naked breeze
Misty kisses tickle
my skin, wet lips
sing silent
through hazy days…
My harem of fairies
play with my hair
Whisking wind
chills sweetly
weak but lifted
totally bare
except for my pendant
on my chest
resting.

IV-6
Gebo

She has offered me
a gift
as I follow her.
She tells me
about partnership--
separateness even as in union--
My path
leads back
to her,
the Divine.
inside
everything...

IV-7
Mannaz Reversed

In silence
see the enemy
hiding
blind
inside.

Wake up
and see again
the beginning.

IV-8
Wunjo Reversed

Tomorrow brings clarity
A much needed light
To see the crisis
with tranquil might.

IV-9
Berkana Reversed

Diligence
Not dismay
with time
it will grow

Preparations
beneath the birch tree
in cultivated soil

A picture of my action
peace with daytime life.

IV-10
Raido

I privately heal
during my journey
to find
that peace of mind
had lost
before this becoming.

V In The End, There Was Just One

V-1
Stringless Bikini

I considered writing a poem
About this one guy I know—
I'm with him in a sexy glance—
a vision of a few nights past—
and a wanting
for more…

I just might follow him…
to our own created shores…
Private moments
teeter
on the totter of my mind.
I walk the halls
blind to all,
except my thoughts…

his behind…

his masculine gentleness
a scent
so sweet
of pleasure and peace
I thirst
release

into the arms
of that passion
I find…

move with me
roll with me
climb me
until you reach…
until you peak…
and I promise…

You will fly.

I cannot get lost
I am balancing my life
I feel it in my jeans
As they fall from my hips,
Slip down my thighs…
I feel it in a dark corner
Within a simple kiss
A craving comes over me
But I walk on
Cool and kind
I could write for days and days
But 'd rather live my life
I'll do it while I rhyme
I do not dare analyze
I do not care to think at all
Today is his

Today is mine.
For now,
Good night.

Case No. 2004CM55555

In bong drift daze...

Life's song has two beats, stupidity wreaks havoc on a broken soul.

Love is or isn't times two times three time keeps creeping-- a ghoulish treat.

Unusual truths do peak through, but it's okay, keep hidden away, be cool.

Sense it all dancing with the sweetest mango and the softest horizon flashing paranoid,

grim.

In a daydream screaming monotone disguising voices within the same brain--

On and on rocking to beats tasting so sweet—and hair like a crystal river.

Numbing music caressing with whispers and piano pleasures...

Victim to addiction

Sobriety

Remembering the pleasant things and not forgetting to brush your teeth.

Energy comes naturally, while tasting strawberry covered crepes...

Another chore done with time to live, meditate, or dance a jig...

Love someone, and exercise with reggae guy—stretched out thighs…
Improvise, keep it wise.
Timely, precisely take the time, lest ye be victim to the sober dream.
Yesterdays gone—try not to scream.

V-3
The Ring

The need to write a poem pushes this pen--
I guide right in to the pleasing remedy.
Life's ironies exert their forces
I rebound in a dance of discrepancy.

The unspoken language I welcome to my knowledge…
Incautious, I become overwhelmed—ceased.
And again it is escape I seek—mind altering, losing,
Back to the beginning of another ring.

V-4
A Note:

Hi It's me.
I'm burning your *Digable Planet* CD.
I just wrote a poem—
I can't stop rhyming.
I have this need—
This need to speak.
I'm drunk, I'm stumped,
Please listen to me.
You won't get your notebook.
You won't get me.
I think you're a player,
But why lie to me?
You should know I was okay
With the truth and the play,
But you told me things
I didn't want to hear…
You acted like there was
Much more there.
If you didn't front,
I wouldn't feel like a chump,
But now I'm lost
And now you're dumped.
It could have been cool…
It could have been sweet…
These four months were fun,
But I will not weep.

My walls are still up,
Lucky for me.
See I'm not strong enough
To be your lady.
I don't know what it is you need,
But I realize—you don't need me.
Your exgirlfriends you miss—
Too much pleasure that you wish—
So please, I ask, just let me be.
I'm sorry but
I can't handle the stress,
And I need to get this
Off of my chest.
It probably
Wouldn't have worked anyway
So we're off again.
Please don't freak.
I know I have issues,
And you're too much for me.
Peace
see, I hope we can be
sweet friends
In the end.
Blessings to you.
-from me.

V-5
Breathless Vibes

Slide your body
into mine
Beneath the rain
Dance with my
Everything
Feel the flight

Let me take you in
We start the climb—
waves—flashes—
I'll be kind.
The rain moves
with spinning grind…
I'm here with you
Closer still
Feel everything
Open wide—
With our energy
Take my ride
Midnight treat
November night—

Jump me sweet
I wrap my thighs
Rain on me
Let me hear your voice.

You feel my heat
I squeeze you tight
We fall asleep
to breathless vibes.

V-6
Psychic Bondage of Three Women

You told her, didn't you?
That demon who befriends
like the mother of lies.
That disturbed one
sick with deeds that defy.
I must tell you, truly,
that I do not curse.
As you know already,
I just break the ties.

V-7
The Witching Hour

Kitten warmth in knitted blankets
Claws like ice "Wake up!"
White beam through window screen
Shining emeralds in the night
What is that you say?
The day hasn't yet begun.
"The moon is full
bind the foe,"
purrs nocturnal feline

like music giving spirit
without any lies…

I descend unto my patio
The rays I cast
with moonbeams dance
as I ask for her protection
so mote it be
amen.

V-8
Phantom Lives, a song

I lay naked
On my beach of white
Sliding past
Another life…

I don't wanna be a whore
Even if you are!
I don't wanna be a whore
Even if you are!
If you were here
I would not hide
But you're with her
Am I fucking blind?!

When you're here
I do not try
Naturally
I ride the tides

The Sun releases
Smoke sweet pipe
To taste the green
To just feel Right!

I don't wanna be a whore
Even if you are!

I don't wanna be a whore
Even if you are!
If you were here
I would not hide
But you're with her
Am I fucking blind?!

I cannot see
Past the next line
You are here
My crazy guide

I'm on you
To make you cry
Rock your world
Until it's time

All is gone
But flesh and thighs
You crush my mind
Shock my insides!

I don't wanna be a whore
Even if you are!
I don't wanna be a whore
Even if you are!
If you were here
I would not hide
But you're with her

Am I fucking blind?!

The day has dawned
I wake up twice
When dusk comes
I will be fine.

I'm thirty-five
Decades pass by
But through it all
I've stayed alive!

Round and round
on another high
Then off we go
toward phantom lives

I'm on my own
And it feels right
We do not share
Our phantom lives

I don't wanna be a whore
Even if you are!
I don't wanna be a whore
Even if you are!
If you were here
I would not hide
But you're with her

Am I fucking blind?!

Tomorrow's gone
Embrace the light
Drift on through
Into night

Morning After Union Station

A March morning, taunting
with light at play, dancing
Cigarette smoke spirals
with currents of wind.

The horizon beckons
welcoming Sunday rising
pretty maidens
out from hiding
Sleepy eyes opening
to the sparkle of a child's grin.

I pull out into the street
past the brick painted sign
about poverty--
a need to be kind.

In this community
The churchgoers stroll
in beautiful clothes
a formal time
this day, this week.

I continue my drive
past golden walk signs
that stand beneath the trees--

Cast iron doorways
and vacant lots lead
to the corner
above the tunnels
echoing out about
the wet debris.

Ahead, a man selling
newspapers wrapped in plastic
I wisp past dormant branches
turn my radio in tune--
soft soul music soothes
The earth whispers
warm wind cools
the church bells ring
the gospel grooves.

The trees cast their patterns
across cracked pavement
hued with tar stains.
My tires splash through--
I exit the city
by way of the current
the interstate guiding
to wherever I choose.

Note #2, June

I know you miss my body
Workin on my Hottie
You and Me--
Doin the naughty.

When we were together we
were givin each other pleasure
Be it talk about the weather
Or you singin me your measures...

hmmm... my flexibility...

Hey-- Fuck it
You lost me.

I Wish Him Peace, As I Bleed

I need to be refilled
just a little bit at least
I can probably
build on from there...

It's this lovin
see
or maybe
a need for
prayer

I have a rhythm
I'd like to share
but he hears a different song
and I'm not there

Wait a minute
a moment or two
I think
I can produce
with this pen
an energy
that little bit
needed to start
words--electric--
from within my broken heart

here I bleed
but possibly maybe
I'll create a cure
to stop the pain
It's been a year
Now he remains
just a memory...
it won't fade away.

V-12
Friday Night

Listless cravings
Didactic days
Smashing my branded skull
Into the face of the sun
Drinking on
Hazy sorrow

A faint ticking
Graying reminder
Reading eyes
Closing behind me
As I suffocate myself
Breathless
Stillness sedates me
I am numb
Feeling outside myself
Distorting
Picasso pieces
Jumbling
Trying to be seen
Until time finds me
And cravings sneak upon me
Lungs full
Teeth clean
Beer in one hand
A joint in my jeans...

Ah, I should go for a walk.

But I don't have a dog.

Sleep it off
The earth breathes on
as I do.

Good night.

V-13
Muse

Could it be it was you all along?
Or am I stuck in the same helpless song?
Year after year doomed to endure
guaranteed sorrow saved for tomorrow.
I don't want to go into some dream—
A dream is a dream is a dream is a dream.
In the end you see reality
Is actually the easier way of living.

Hope is accepted within my truths—
Because now I know my control is merely my mood.

Possibly maybes are just what they say
possibly maybe it will go away.

Oh— I know better
Or maybe I don't…
I'm so clueless…
Is it all a joke?
Do we all find a niche?
Or are there a few souls
who wander around
in their endless woes?

I'm thirty-one—
Soon to be thirty-two—

I must say this loud—
I'm glad to find you!
sober and happy
Alive
with peace.
Embrace your life--
your will, it's growing.

I climb a new mountain
But I'm not lost anymore.
I know what I have
This day—this hour—
Myself, and my cat!
and my hope for
tomorrow!

V-14
Searching for the Highest Clouds

My solitude
is the result of my survival

My fear
is the loss of my youth

My womanhood
is the peak of the mountaintop
past the valley paths
below the next climb

Why do I cry?
praying for serenity
searching for the highest clouds.

Currents Of Wind Surfing On Silver Rain

He crushed on Me
I let it ride
Enjoying him
Asking Why

Currents of wind surfing
on silver rain

The circle closes--
a new one begins.
The moon is waxing
The future-- grim.

I like to f-   him
and it's not a sin
but I fear this boy
might fall in

I cannot keep him
It won't last long
Should I warn him
or ride the storm?

V-16
Warming Up After Being Stoned Cold

He was
my hot spring
Waking me out
from my daze
Coating my soul
with what I'd lost
Never breaking my heart
Never giving me his
We chose to part
Now I look back
I see
I fell in love
with him and me.

V-17
Old Friend

We partied like a frat house
We dance until dawn
Nothing could stop us
When we were young

But the bottle took you
The pipe took me
you are drowning
my lungs unclean

In your silence, find your soul
In my quiet, I'll retire my bowl
Remember high school
our priorities
They did not include
the mind warping...

V-18
Strength

Seeking
around the ashes
Discovering
new sight
I found
Love
as it is in my century.

Made in the USA
Monee, IL
30 April 2023

32618846R00056